A gift for:

Tiffany

From:

Diane & Brady

2011

Copyright © 2009 Hallmark Licensing, Inc.

Published by Hallmark Books,
a division of Hallmark Cards, Inc.,
Kansas City, MO 64141
Visit us on the Web at www.Hallmark.com.

Editor: Megan Langford
Art Director: Kevin Swanson
Designer: Mark Voss
Production Artist: Dan Horton

ISBN: 978-1-59530-244-1

BOK2102

Printed and bound in China

FOUR SEASONS OF FUN

PRACTICALLY FREE THINGS FOR FAMILIES TO DO TOGETHER

BY STACEY NICHOLS KIM

Winter

Spring

Summer

Fall

Foreword

52 weeks, 365 days, 8,760 hours, or 525,600 minutes in a year . . . no matter how you count it, that's a lot of time! Don't let all that time pass you and your family by. Start making your together-time count with activities that kids and parents alike will love. From making homemade pretzels to volunteering at an animal shelter, these activities won't just be a way to pass the time on a Saturday afternoon. You'll be making memories that'll last a lifetime.

SWIRLING SNOWFLAKES, HOT COCOA, AND WOOLEN MITTENS . . .

It must be winter!

Baby, it's cold outside! Snowy days and blustery nights mean families often spend their time holed up indoors, lazing around and wishing for warmer weather. But just because the days are shorter, that's no reason to not have fun. There are plenty of activities that you and your family can do together that don't require sunshine or eighty-degree weather. And the best part? They don't require a lot of cash, either.

TIME IN A BOTTLE
MAKING A TIME CAPSULE

COST: **FREE-$**

MATERIALS: box

For adults, time seems to pass by so quickly. A year can go by in the blink of an eye. For kids, time moves more slowly—they wonder if summer will ever come, if that loose tooth will ever fall out, or if their age will ever be expressed in double digits.

Making a time capsule is a fun way for adults and kids to see how much happens in a family's year. The container you use does not have to be fancy. An old shoebox, a plastic bin, or even a grocery bag will make a fine time capsule. Just be sure to pick something big enough to hold all of your treasures!

You can include anything you want in your capsule, but it's most fun to pack away things that mark milestones that allow you to see change over a year's time.

If you're feeling especially creative and you have the right tools, you can include videos, home movies, or digital slideshows of your life right now.

HERE ARE SOME IDEAS FOR YOUR TIME CAPSULE:

- current family photos (don't forget your pets!)
- a list of favorite books and songs
- a package of a favorite snack
- a recent drawing or work of art
- a favorite piece of clothing that is getting too small
- a picture of a favorite toy
- pictures of your home and car
- a chart of "vital statistics" for each family member (height, weight, etc.)

Each family member can also include a list of predictions. You could make a list titled "By next year I will have . . ." and then fill in the blanks.

Once you have gathered all of your items, put them in your container and seal it up. Kids love to cover things with glue and tape, so go crazy! You can decorate the box and put a label on it warning that it is not to be opened until a certain date. Find a not-too-secret hiding place for the box and tuck it away. If you have a family calendar, mark the date on which your time capsule will be opened. Now all you have to do is wait . . .

MATERIALS: maple syrup (about ¼ c. per person), clean snow (or crushed/shaved ice), shallow dishes or pans (1 per person—pie plates work well), heavy pot, forks

Who doesn't love the warm, comforting taste of maple syrup? Here is a fun alternative to eating it on pancakes and waffles.

If you live in a place where it snows a lot, you can gather clean, fresh snow to use for this activity. If it doesn't snow where you live or you can't find clean snow, that's OK. You can make your own "snow" by crushing ice in a blender or putting ice cubes in layers of plastic baggies and crushing it with a hammer or mallet. Gathering or making the snow is part of the fun!

Fill one pie plate or other shallow dish per person with snow. You need to have these dishes at the ready, but you don't want the snow to melt. Keep them in the freezer or outside until you have completed the next step. Place the maple syrup into a heavy pot. Kids love to help measure and pour, so be sure to let them in on the action. (Remember—use ¼ cup per person.) Depending on your kids' ages, count out how many measures of syrup you need or talk about how many quarter cups make one cup. Heat the syrup over medium heat, stirring near-constantly, until it reaches a rolling boil and starts to thicken.

Set your dishes of snow out in a row on a counter or table. The syrup will be very hot, so have children stand back while you pour. Drizzle hot syrup over each dish of snow. It should not sink in but rather form a sticky, taffy-like candy on the snow's surface that everyone can twirl onto a fork and eat almost like spaghetti.

Sugar-on-snow is traditionally eaten with sour pickles and plain doughnuts to cut the candy's sweetness. No matter how you choose to eat it, *bon appétit!*

WANT TO PERSONALIZE YOUR DISHES?
EACH FAMILY MEMBER CAN USE FOOD COLORING TO TINT HIS OR HER SNOW A FAVORITE COLOR.

Turn your house into a winter wonderland with snowflakes and garlands aplenty. To make a snowflake, you will need one square sheet of paper. Use the traditional white or mix it up with colored construction paper. The most simple way to make the snowflakes is to fold the paper in half, making a rectangle, then fold it again to make a square, then fold it on the diagonal to make a triangle. Trim and cut the paper, then unfold to reveal your creation.

The more paper you cut away, the "lacier" your snowflakes will be. Older children with well-developed scissor skills might want to look up detailed paper snowflake patterns on the Internet. Completed snowflakes will be beautiful as they are, but can also be decorated with glitter or sequins. Hang the snowflakes in windows, on the walls, or from the ceiling.

Garlands are another simple winter craft that delight kids of all ages. Set out bowls of the traditional popcorn and cranberries for kids to string, or experiment with other options such as pasta or small beads. You may need to help kids thread the needles and tie a knot at the end of the string. Encourage children to experiment with patterns as they make their garland. Hang the garlands in windows and doorways or from light fixtures and mantels.

For younger children who are not ready to handle a needle and thread, paper chains are a good alternative to stringing garlands. To begin, cut construction paper into strips. The paper can be left plain or decorated with markers, crayons, glitter, or stickers. To start the chain, use a glue stick to attach the ends of one strip together, forming a loop. Hook the next strip through the loop and attach the ends. Continue in this way until the chain is as long as desired.

✳ PAPER CHAINS CAN BE USED TO COUNT DOWN THE DAYS TO A SIGNIFICANT EVENT SUCH AS A BIRTHDAY OR OTHER CELEBRATION—SIMPLY REMOVE ONE STRIP FROM THE CHAIN PER DAY.

PAPER SNOWFLAKE DIAGRAM:

FOLD

CUT

UNFOLD

HERE'S WHAT TO DO:

1. Fold the paper in half, making a rectangle.
2. Fold it again to make a square.
3. Fold it on the diagonal, to make a triangle.
4. Trim and cut the paper.
5. Unfold to reveal your creation.

Old, broken, stubby crayons pile up just like the last little bits of bars of soap. But even crayons that have become too short for little fingers to hold can be given new life.

Kids of all ages can enjoy making rainbow crayons. Preheat your oven to 250°F. Place muffin papers in muffin tins. Make sure that all paper has been removed from the crayon scraps, then select five to ten different colored crayon bits to place in each cup. Place the tins in the oven. Kids will love turning on the oven light and watching the crayons melt together. Once the crayons have melted, remove the tins from the oven and let cool before peeling off the muffin papers and making masterpieces with your creations.

You can also melt crayons in a glass container in the microwave, then layer the melted colors for a true rainbow effect. If you have them around the house, you can also use other containers, such as candy molds, heart-shaped muffin tins, or silicone ice-cube trays as molds.

Let your imagination run wild and see who can come up with the wackiest combination of colors. Use your completed crayons to make pictures for a family art gallery to be hung on the fridge, in the hallway, or in any other high-traffic area in the house. Your pictures can have a theme (portraits, still life, etc.) or can simply be artist's choice. Encourage all budding Picassos to write a title and description of each work to hang next to it, just like in a museum.

❋ FOR A DENSER MIX OF COLORS, OLDER CHILDREN CAN USE THE LARGE HOLES ON A BOX GRATER TO GRATE THE CRAYONS INTO THE MUFFIN CUPS.

It can be difficult for children to look beyond what they have in order to think about what others might lack. At the same time, children care deeply about the welfare of others. Making the time to volunteer as a family is a rewarding experience that teaches children compassion, helps them to appreciate the good things in their lives, and provides an opportunity to talk about giving and sharing.

If your family has never undertaken a volunteer opportunity before, you can start small and local. Look around your neighborhood. What could you do to help? If inclement weather makes it hard for an elderly neighbor to take his dog out for a walk, volunteer to take over that task for him. If it snows where you live, shovel your neighbor's walk after the next storm—even if that's something she could do for herself. Making soup for supper? Deliver some to the people next door. If you don't know your neighbors very well, this is a great way to meet them and build community. As winter turns to spring, see if anyone needs help with yard work.

You're likely to find that when you start giving, you just want to give more. Once you've done some volunteering in the neighborhood, you can spread your wings and look for other ways to get involved. See if local homeless shelters need help serving holiday meals. If your children are too young to dish up food, you can collect toys, toiletries, blankets, and non-perishable food to give to shelters. Kids are often particularly motivated to help other kids, so if there are any family shelters in your area, see what you can do for them.

The Internet is a wonderful resource for volunteer opportunities and ideas. Check the web for ways you can help from a distance if the opportunities in your town are limited. You could, for example, be a pen pal to an elderly person, a sick child, or a soldier deployed overseas. The ways to help are unlimited—just like the good feelings you get from paying it forward.

6 SNOW SPRAY PAINTING

COST: FREE

MATERIALS: food coloring, water, spray bottles, large sheets of paper (optional)

Next time you look out the window and see a snow-covered lawn, try not to think, "Another day stuck inside." Instead, see the snow as a blank canvas waiting for your artistic touch.

To make fabulous works of snow art, you'll first need to create your paints. Mix water and food coloring in spray bottles until you've mixed your perfect shades. For best results, make the colors fairly dark. Then simply bundle up and head outside with your bottles of paint.

You can spray abstract designs on the snow or create a mural of a specific scene. It might be fun to paint a beach scene or flower garden to bring warm thoughts to the cold day. Or create an entire zoo of painted animals right in your own backyard! If your creation gets covered up by the next snowfall, just go back out and paint again.

If you live somewhere that doesn't get snow, don't let that stop you from making spray art. You can do the same project outdoors on a large piece of paper. (Tear a sheet from a roll of newsprint or tape together a number of smaller sheets to get a piece of paper big enough for your art.)

✳ BE CAREFUL! THE FOOD COLORING CAN STAIN CLOTHING, FENCES, AND OTHER MATERIALS.

For families living in cold climates, winter can cause a serious case of cabin fever. Even those who can play outside year-round face days of being stuck inside if it rains. One way to channel the endless amounts of physical energy that homebound kids possess is to let them climb the walls—almost literally—on an in-home obstacle course.

Obstacles can be set up as stations that move progressively through the house. The options are endless.

IDEAS FOR YOUR INDOOR PLAYGROUND:

- Drape a sheet over a dining-room table to create a tunnel to crawl through.
- Crawl over or under the dining-room chairs that were moved to make the tunnel.
- Make a "hot lava" zone in a large, open area. Tape down pieces of paper to serve as safe zones; hop from paper to paper to avoid the lava and get across the room. If a foot gets "burned," it's back to the beginning.
- Place a hula-hoop (or large loop of string) on the floor and jump into and out of the circle a set number of times.
- Jump rope for the duration of a song.
- Use a laundry basket for a beanbag toss; make a certain number of "baskets" before moving on to the next station.
- Walk the length of a hallway with a book or other object balanced on top of the head.
- Tape a piece of string to the floor in a straight line or zigzag pattern the length of the hall; walk this "balance beam."

Involve kids in setting up the course and coming up with ideas to keep it challenging. If kids seem bored after a few times through the course, there are plenty of ways to keep things fresh. Start by rearranging or modifying the stations. Challenge kids to complete the course while wearing a large, floppy hat; if the hat falls off, it's back to the beginning. Another fun challenge is to try to do as many things on the course as possible backwards—including going through the stations in reverse order.

Don't forget that this obstacle course is not just for kids. The fun will last longer if the whole family participates. Seeing mom or dad try to cross the "hot lava" zone is sure to make everyone laugh.

Making a jigsaw puzzle is a simple and satisfying activity that can easily be adapted for children of various ages. Puzzles are best when made from lightweight material such as cereal boxes that were destined for the recycling. (Corrugated cardboard tends to be too heavy and difficult to cut unless a very simple puzzle pattern is planned.)

Flatten your box then cut off the flaps until you have a large, flat surface. Use markers or crayons to draw a picture on the blank side of the cardboard. Alternatively, draw the picture on a sheet of paper, then glue the paper to the cardboard. You could also print out a family photo or other image to use as the puzzle picture. Once the image is completed and glued down (if necessary), flip the cardboard over and use a marker to draw the puzzle pattern on the back. Larger, simpler pieces will make easier puzzles while smaller, more intricate pieces will be more difficult to put together. For a real challenge, cut your puzzle into uniform squares—that way, the shape of the pieces provides no clues at all!

When the pieces have all been cut, put those puzzles together! Everyone can do the puzzle that he or she creates, but it's more fun to trade. Afterward, zip-top bags are perfect for storing the puzzle pieces. If the puzzle's image is a printout of a photograph or other picture, include an additional printout to use as a guide in the bag with the pieces. If the puzzle is an original work of art, consider taking a picture of it before cutting it up, then making a printout of the image to serve as the map.

For more puzzle fun, make a letter puzzle. As a family, write a letter to a friend or relative. Glue the letter onto cardboard and cut it up into a puzzle. Mail the pieces to the lucky recipient. After all, who wouldn't want to receive a puzzle letter?

The short days of winter make it an excellent season for stargazing since the sun sets long before bedtime. Don't let cold temperatures deter you, either. Pile on the layers, bring an insulated container of hot chocolate and a bag of cookies, and prepare to be dazzled by the twinkling lights up above.

Stargazing is best done away from the ambient light of neighborhood streetlights or the haze of a city's glow. You'll need a star map, which you can find online for free. A flashlight with a strong beam will help to point out the stars as you find them.

Before you set out on your adventure, you might want to do some research about the meaning of the constellations you will see. The Big Dipper is the formation that is likely to be most familiar and easy to pick out in the night sky. The dipper's real name is Ursa Major, or the Great Bear. The dipper's handle represents the bear's tail, much different from a modern-day bear's short stub. The star in the bend of the Big Dipper's handle is actually two stars, Mizar and Alcor, that appear so close together that they look like one.

The two stars that form the edge of the Big Dipper's bowl furthest away from the handle will point you to Polaris, the North Star. To find Cassiopeia, locate the second star in the Big Dipper's handle and make a straight line from this star to Polaris. Just beyond Polaris you will find Cassiopeia, in the shape of a W or M depending on the season. Continue on your trajectory past Cassiopeia to find the Great Square of Pegasus, the flying horse.

If your stargazing expedition creates some budding astronomers and your city or town has an observatory or a planetarium, check to see if they offer free or low-cost programs. Perhaps family stargazing will become a weekly event during which you can discover and learn about a new constellation each time.

Going out to eat is one of life's greatest pleasures, but also a big expense for a family. With a little advance planning, you can create the magic of the restaurant experience right in your own home. Parents become the wait staff and chefs and kids become the esteemed guests.

Start by setting a lovely table complete with a tablecloth, candles, cloth napkins, and the good china. Set as many places as you have children—this is their special "night out." Plan a menu of their favorite foods, offering two choices each for appetizer, main course, side dish, and dessert. You may want to prepare as many items in advance as possible so that when dinnertime rolls around, a few minutes in the microwave are all that will be required.

Encourage children to wear fancy clothes for dinner, but be prepared for spills. Show children to their seats and either present them with menus or read them a list of choices. Get into the spirit by wearing an apron and taking orders on a notepad.

MAKE DINNER EXTRA FUN BY:

- playing special dinner music.
- putting a basket of bread or rolls on the table with little pats of butter.
- providing individual condiments, such as ketchup in small bottles or miniature jars of jam.
- serving a special beverage, such as sparkling cider or chocolate milk.
- presenting children with a bill at the end of the meal and allowing them to "pay."

If you have older children who enjoy testing their culinary wings, let them turn the tables and serve you. You can help them plan the menu and set the table. Many children will enjoy the opportunity to be in charge and assume the adult role of server and chef. You can also serve and be served in child/adult groupings so that children aren't left alone with the run of the kitchen!

Working together to cook and serve a meal is another way to have fun family time with the restaurant theme. If your family enjoys ethnic food, learn how to cook your favorites at home. Research together the ingredients needed and the preparation involved, then enjoy the meal as a family.

Cell phones, the Internet, computer games, TV, MP3 players, PDAs, portable DVD players . . . being wired is a part of life in the twenty-first century. Kids and parents spend increasing amounts of time in front of screens and using various electronic devices. This 24/7 interconnectivity somehow manages to both bring us all closer together as well as push us into our own individual e-worlds.

Take a day as a family to unplug and recharge. Disconnecting for a day is a great way to focus on spending time as a family with minimal distractions. Decide as a family how "disconnected" you want to be. Do you want to answer the phone? Use the car? Turn on the lights? It's up to you.

This should be a fun activity—not something that's done under duress. Don't worry if you want to listen to music while you do a certain activity or if you need to look up the recipe for dinner online. Just have fun, focus on being together, and be creative about alternatives to plugging in. At the end of the day, talk about what you liked and disliked about minimizing technology for a day. Maybe unplugging will become a regular event!

HERE ARE SOME WAYS TO PASS
THE UNPLUGGED TIME:

- Take turns reading aloud to each other.
- Play board and card games.
- Walk to nearby places you usually drive to.
- Have a candlelight dinner.
- Get out the art supplies and make a family collage.
- Write a progressive story: each person writes one line then passes it along to the next person.
- Clean out your closets. Who knows what forgotten treasures you'll discover?
- Look through old photo albums together.
- Make cards for friends and family who live far away.

Skiers and snowboaders love dry, powdery snow. But those who love making snowballs, snowforts, and snowmen will want the kind of snow that's wet and sticky. If you wake up to find the ground covered with perfect snowman-making snow, don't let it go to waste! Bundle up and get outside—it's time to make snowmen!

For a change of pace, don't just limit yourself to making snowmen. You can make snowwomen, snowchildren, snowfamilies . . . the possibilities are practically endless. Snowpeople don't have to be three stacked snowballs, either. Try building long and lean or short and stout. You might even build a snowman who is standing on his head or a snowwoman who is reclining against a snowy bank. Maybe each member of the family will want to build their own likeness in snow.

If snowpeople aren't appealing, maybe you will be interested in creating snow animals! A snowball on the ground quickly becomes a porcupine when you add twigs to its back. Wet snow can easily be sculpted into turtles, ladybugs, or snakes. More advanced snow carvers might want to attempt dogs and cats. Let your imagination run wild!

Once your snow creature is in place, add hats, scarves, and mittens on sticks to give it some character. Carrots make great noses, and buttons will work for eyes. To create button eyes that will stay put when the snow begins to melt, thread a pipe cleaner through each button and insert the button eyes into each head. You can also use pipe cleaners to secure props for your snow creatures, like a snow shovel, sunglasses, or a bow tie.

When your snow creations are complete, take photos. You never know how long they'll last once the sun warms things up!

Don't let winter get you down! An indoor family pool party is a great way to combat winter blahs. Even if you live somewhere with good weather all year round, the novelty of bringing an outdoor party inside will put a smile on everyone's face.

Dig out your swimsuits, goggles, and flip-flops. Put on your favorite summertime tunes. There are lots of fun activities to do!

YOU COULD:

- splash around in the tub while wearing swimsuits. Don't forget the shovels, buckets, and other beach toys!
- race rubber duckies from one end of the tub to the other.
- go on a "flip-flop hunt." Take turns hiding one of each family member's flip-flops, then having everyone search for his or her match.
- do the limbo in the living room. How low can you go?

In lieu of making sand castles, have fun playing with "goo" made from cornstarch and water. Mix 2 cups cornstarch with 1 cup water in a large bowl and see what happens! When you're done playing, wrap up in beach towels and have a snack. Everyone is sure to be hungry! Serve summertime favorites such as fruit punch, frozen grapes, and ice cream sandwiches. Spend the rest of the day dressed in shorts, T-shirts, hats, and sunglasses.

BLOOMING FLOWERS, RAIN SHOWERS, AND RED ROBINS . . .

It must be spring!

. . . .

After a long winter, warmer weather is finally here. Just as the buds are ready to stretch toward the sun and baby birds are ready to learn to fly, families can't wait to rediscover each other and the world around them. Everybody wants to get moving and get outside! These activities will have you and your family laughing, playing, and even learning— all while barely spending a dime.

The first warm days of spring are perfect for heading outdoors to enjoy the delightful mess of homemade bubbles. The best part? Bubbles are easy to make.

HERE IS A BASIC BUBBLE RECIPE:

- ½ gallon water
- ½ cup dishwashing liquid
- ¼ cup light corn syrup

You can use regular tap water for your bubbles, but if your water is from a well or is especially hard, the bubbles will be less sturdy. You can get around this by using distilled water. And why corn syrup? The thick, sticky syrup makes the walls of your bubbles thicker, stronger, and slower to dry out. If you don't have any corn syrup on hand, substitute 1 tablespoon of white sugar instead. Try not to shake up your solution too much while mixing it as it is harder to blow big bubbles when the liquid is foamy.

Don't limit yourself to regular old bubbles. Add a few drops of liquid food coloring to make colored bubbles. Just be careful since these can stain hands, clothing, and anything they land on. Encourage children to catch colored bubbles on white paper. When the bubbles pop, they will create beautiful and unique works of art.

If you can't find any bubble wands, lots of household objects will work. Make any shape you want by bending pipe cleaners or coat hangers into wands. Strawberry baskets and fly swatters (clean, of course!) will make lots of little, tiny bubbles. Metal cookie cutters work well for forming bubbles, too.

To make the biggest, best bubbles, don't put your mouth too close to the wand, don't blow too hard, and twist your wrist to release your creation from the wand. With a little practice, everyone in the family will be bubble experts in no time.

YOU CAN USE YOUR BUBBLE SOLUTION THE SAME DAY YOU MAKE IT,
BUT IT ACTUALLY WORKS BEST AFTER IT RESTS FOR A FEW DAYS.

15 A-TISKET, A-TASKET
MAKING A FLOWER BASKET

COST: $

MATERIALS: construction paper, berry baskets, empty 20-oz. or 2-liter soda bottles, hole punch, box cutter or craft knife, ribbon, wire, scissors, glue

A basket full of flowers is a great way to celebrate the arrival of spring. Kids of all ages can create simple baskets to fill with real or paper flowers.

For the youngest members of the family, make a basket by simply twisting a piece of construction paper into a cone and securing it with glue or tape. Cones can be made tall and narrow or short and wide. Trim the top of the cone to even it out. Punch holes on opposite sides of the cone's mouth and add a ribbon or wire handle. These baskets look great hanging from doorknobs.

Collect plastic berry baskets for a slightly more advanced activity. Kids can weave colorful ribbon or strips of construction paper through the basket's holes. Make a handle out of ribbon or lightweight cardboard (simply cut a strip from an old cereal box).

With a little help, older kids can turn old soda bottles into spring baskets. An adult should cut the top of the bottle off with a box cutter or craft knife, about four inches from the base. Punch holes on opposite sides of the basket's mouth and add a ribbon or wire handle. If you have a hot glue gun, you can use it to decorate the plastic basket with old buttons, fabric scraps, pom-poms, or anything else you can think of. You can also draw on the plastic with permanent marker.

Baskets can be filled with paper flowers made from tissue or construction paper and pipe cleaners or fresh-picked flowers from your yard. Decorate your own home with your creations, or continue the long-standing May Day tradition of surprising your neighbors. On May first, hang a basket of real or paper flowers on a neighbor's doorknob, then ring the bell and run away. Don't get caught! The identity of the giver should remain a surprise, although you can attach a card or note wishing the recipient a happy spring from a secret admirer.

Making butter is incredibly simple and almost magical. Start with a liquid and end with a solid? You bet.

All you need to make butter is some heavy cream. Really—that's it! Put the cream in a container with a tight-fitting lid and shake it up. Whatever container you use, you'll want to fill it about half full with cream so that there's plenty of room for the liquid to slosh around while you're shaking. A larger container with a large amount of cream will take longer to solidify than a smaller container with a small amount of cream. Children might enjoy having their own individual containers to shake (baby food jars work well), or you can pass one larger container around and take turns. All that shaking is hard work, and everyone might appreciate a break.

You'll need to shake the cream for 10–20 minutes before the butter forms. Pass the time by putting on some music and dancing around while you shake the jar. Once the butter has formed, drain out the liquid buttermilk (which can be used for drinking or cooking) and enjoy your homemade butter on a slice of bread or a cracker.

Homemade butter is delicious on its own, but you can also add flavorings like a pinch of salt, fresh or dried herbs, honey and chopped walnuts, or cinnamon and sugar. After you drain off the liquid, mix your flavorings in well then refrigerate your butter until firm. You can even put your soft butter in candy molds to make fun shapes like roses or hearts. Homemade butter is a great treat to share with family and friends.

Why limit dinner to the dining room or kitchen? Make your evening meal more fun by having a meal that progresses through the house.

Choose three or four locations in the house that are not the norm for family dining then eat each course in a different spot. You could put a blanket on the floor of the living room for a picnic feel, or put placemats on the coffee table and sit cross-legged in front of your food. If the weather is good enough, a table in the yard would be a fun stop. Does your house have stairs? Use them as seats!

Plan your menu carefully. Since you'll be eating in unusual and potentially precarious settings, you'll want to avoid messy items—no soup or spaghetti! A simple meal with a starter of cheese and crackers, a main course of sandwiches, and a third course of cut fruit would be just fine. The novelty of this fun dining experience means no one will be too concerned with what's on the menu. Consider ending the meal in the family room with cookies and milk in front of a favorite movie. Or, if you have a fireplace, gas range, or outdoor fire pit, s'mores make an excellent ending to your dining journey.

Planting a seed, tending it, and watching a plant grow are fascinating activities for children. Here are a couple of simple seed-sprouting activities that you can do at home. A fun activity for kids of all ages is to plant grass seeds in empty eggshells.

HERE'S WHAT YOU NEED TO KNOW:

1. Carefully crack eggs so that the top third or so of the shell comes off, leaving the bottom two-thirds as a small, open container.
2. Wash the shells out carefully. Children can use a permanent marker to draw a face on the shell. When the grass sprouts, it will look like hair!
3. Place the shells in an empty egg carton and fill them with potting soil.
4. Sprinkle grass seeds on top and gently press the seeds into the soil.
5. Using a spray bottle, water gently, being careful that the soil does not get soggy.

Within a few days, your creations should sprout hair. Let it grow long or trim it back. Kids will have fun giving their grass-heads names and special hairdos.

A more involved activity is to give seed planting a purpose by sprouting vegetable plants indoors. Vegetables such as lettuce, peppers, and tomatoes can be started in egg cartons or small paper cups.

When the seeds have sprouted, move them to a sunny place and continue to water as necessary. When the plants are three to four inches high, transfer them outside to containers or a garden patch. Seeds sprouted in paper egg cartons can be transferred into the ground, egg carton and all. Just snip the cups apart and plant the whole thing. Don't forget to keep watering! If all goes well, you'll be harvesting your bounty when summer comes.

HERE'S HOW TO START YOUR VEGETABLE GARDEN:

1. Fill each well of the egg carton with a bit of potting soil.
2. Use your finger to make a small indentation in the center of each filled well.
3. Add a seed and cover gently.
4. Mist with water to dampen soil.
5. Cover loosely with plastic wrap and set in a dark place for a few days.
6. Check seedlings daily, and mist as needed to keep soil moist.

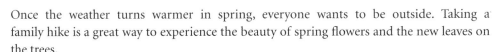

Once the weather turns warmer in spring, everyone wants to be outside. Taking a family hike is a great way to experience the beauty of spring flowers and the new leaves on the trees.

As long as you're not planning to do any serious mountaineering, you don't need any special equipment for a hike. You do need to wear comfortable shoes and dress in layers. And be sure to bring a backpack filled with plenty of water and some healthy snacks.

If there are any state or local parks near your home, go exploring there. Or, keep things closer to home and simply walk around your neighborhood looking for signs of spring. No matter where you decide to hike, it can be fun to make a checklist of things to look for while you're out.

SEE IF YOU CAN SPOT:

- ants
- cats
- dogs
- birds
- an earthworm
- a bird's nest
- a feather
- a spider web
- a pink (or purple or white . . .) flower
- a pinecone
- a rock
- an oak (or maple or evergreen . . .) tree

Modify the list to fit the climate where you live, and be sure to leave a few blank lines for interesting things that you did not expect to see. If you have a camera, take pictures of some of the plants and animals you see. Later, you can identify them using books or the Internet. You can even start a notebook of things that you've seen and found to take on future family hikes.

Local fire stations usually welcome visits from children and their families. And what child wouldn't be thrilled to meet a firefighter and see the engines up close?

Call ahead to find out the best time to visit. Once you have your visit scheduled, you'll want to get prepared. Read books about firefighters to learn more about the important job they do. You may have some books at home already, but if not, the library is a great resource. You can also prepare a list of questions to ask the firefighters during your visit.

HERE'S A LIST TO GET YOU STARTED:

• Why are fire engines red?
• How long are the hoses?
• How do you attach the hoses to the fire hydrants?
• What do you wear to protect you from the fires?
• Is putting out fires your only job, or do you help with other emergencies, too?
• What do you do at the station when there are no fires?
• How many firefighters work at the station?
• What do you like about being a firefighter?

After your visit, make a thank-you card to send to the fire station. Kids may even want to draw a picture showing their trip to include in the card.

 DON'T FORGET TO TAKE A CAMERA AND SNAP PICTURES OF YOUR KIDS WITH THE FIREFIGHTERS!

Going to the park is always fun, but it's easy to get into a routine of going to the same park, be it the one closest to home or the one with the biggest slide. Try a playground crawl to keep the park-lovers in your house happy.

Spend some time scoping out the playgrounds in your area. Elementary schools often have wonderful playgrounds, and if there are any city parks in your area, they might have climbing structures, too. Think outside the box on what could constitute a playground. Some cities have water fountains designed for splashing or town squares with stairs and benches for climbing fun.

Once you have a list of parks, pick three or four, map out the best route, and start your adventure. Be sure to bring a bag of snacks and drinks to fuel you through your park crawl. Spend thirty minutes or so at each park and then move on to the next one. As you drive between destinations, have each family member name his or her favorite and least favorite thing about each location and give it a rating of one to five stars. Maybe you'll find a new favorite!

SAIL AWAY!
BUILDING A BOAT

COST: **$**

MATERIALS: empty paper milk cartons, chopsticks or straws, rubber bands, box cutter or craft knife, duct tape, smaller boxes (such as soap boxes), paper towel or toilet paper tubes, construction paper, permanent markers

Ahoy, mateys! Did you know that your old milk and juice cartons can be turned into boats? It's easy!

HERE'S HOW TO BUILD YOUR BOAT:

1. Rinse your carton out well and tape the spout closed. Lay the carton on its side. The flat end will be the stern (back) of your boat, and the spout end will be the bow (front).
2. Cut away a portion of the top of the boat, exposing the inside of the carton. It's up to you how much you want to cut away—you're the boat builder!
3. Tape a smaller box inside the boat and attach a toilet paper tube to the top as a smokestack.
4. Decorate your boat with flags (use a chopstick or a straw as a flagpole), a sail, or portholes and windows drawn on with permanent marker. Make a pirate ship, an ocean liner, or any kind of boat you like—the possibilities are endless!
5. More advanced boat builders might want to add a rudder. To do so, make two holes at the bottom of the boat's stern. Poke a chopstick through each hole so that about half of the chopstick is inside the boat and half is out. Secure the chopsticks to the inside of the boat with duct tape. Wrap a rubber band around the ends of the chopsticks, and duct tape a flap of the cutaway milk carton to the rubber band. Turn the flap to wind the rubber band around it, then release when you put the boat into the water. The rudder will propel the boat forward.

HERE'S WHERE TO SAIL YOUR BOAT:

1. the bathtub
2. a wading pool
3. a local pond or lake

If you float your boat in a pond, you might want to find a long stick to use to retrieve it if it gets away. Put miniature animals or people or other small treasures in the boat before its send-off.

Anchors aweigh!

(23) **FOR THE BIRDS**
MAKING A SIMPLE BIRD FEEDER

COST: $

MATERIALS: pinecones; peanut butter; birdseed; clean, empty plastic milk jugs or 2-liter soda bottles; sturdy twigs or wooden dowels; box cutter or craft knife; large nail; twine or thin wire

The beautiful colors and graceful movements of birds are fascinating to observe. Try these easy projects to lure feathered friends to your yard.

Kids will love making simple bird feeders from pinecones. To get started, tie a string to the base of the pinecone—large pinecones work best. Coat the pinecone with plain, natural peanut butter, then roll it in birdseed. Hang the cones from tree branches that are visible from inside your home. Then wait for the birds to come. It won't take them long to find their treat!

Milk jugs and 2-liter soda bottles can be reused and made into bird feeders. Use a box cutter to make two large (3- to 4-inch diameter) holes opposite each other about halfway up the sides of the bottle. Use a nail to punch a few holes below each big hole; insert twigs or dowels into these holes to serve as perches. Punch two more holes opposite each other near the top of the bottle and run a length of twine or wire through these two holes to use as a hanger.

Adults should do all the cutting, but kids can help to fill the bottle with seed up to the level of the large holes. Hang your creation from a sturdy branch or hook. Keep the feeder full and soon all the birds in your neighborhood will be stopping by for a meal! Keep a log of the birds you observe at your feeder. If you don't recognize the visitors, take a picture then try to identify them online or in library books. What times of day do the birds like to congregate? What birds visit most frequently?

Everyone has a story to tell. Putting the words on paper and making a simple book can be a powerful—and empowering—experience for even the youngest authors.

The first step for any homemade book is to come up with the story. Do you want to write a true story or a tall tale? A poem, perhaps? While kids are adept at creating fanciful tales of adventure, parents sometimes struggle for ideas. Consider writing a story about something that your children did as infants or toddlers, with the family as characters. Or tell a story from your own childhood—your kids are bound to ask you to read it over and over. You can even work together to write a story as a family. One fun method of collaboration is to write a progressive story. Take turns writing lines until someone brings the story to an end.

Stories can be handwritten or typed on the computer and printed out. An adult can serve as a scribe for kids who are too young to write. Each author should cut the completed story into logical chunks to be glued onto each page. Illustrate each of the book's pages with a drawing, collage, or photo. Don't forget to design a cover that includes the name of the author(s). Covers can be made of cardstock or cardboard to make the finished product more durable.

Depending on the thickness of the book, the simplest way to bind the pages is to gather them together and staple them. You can also hole-punch the pages and either tie them with ribbon or insert them into a three-ring binder. Take turns reading the completed stories to each other and reveling in the power of your collective imagination.

Kids and animals are a natural pairing. Most children love cats, dogs, birds, fish, and all other members of the animal kingdom. Kids also like to help. A love of animals plus a desire to help equals the perfect volunteer opportunity at a local animal shelter or rescue organization!

Finding local groups that need help can be a family activity in and of itself. Look up shelters on the Internet or use the yellow pages. There are even services online that will match you with animal rescue organizations that need volunteers. Once you have found a place to volunteer your time, you might be surprised by the kinds of tasks you can help out with.

SHELTERS NEED HELPERS FOR MANY DIFFERENT THINGS:

- walking dogs
- grooming animals
- cleaning cages
- stuffing envelopes for educational mailings
- playing with pets
- helping at fundraising events

Volunteering with animals can be dirty business, so dress casually and be prepared to work hard. No matter what kind of task you end up helping out with, you're certain to spend part of your time cuddling and loving the adorable pets that live at the shelter. Who will enjoy it more: you or the animals? Everyone wins!

Flying a kite on a bright spring day is an iconic image of childhood. Help your children make their own kites to make the experience even more special.

You can start a very simple kite with just four craft sticks. Glue them together in a diamond shape. Glue a chopstick between two corners to make a crossbar. When the glue on the frame is dry, trace the outline of the frame onto waxed paper or construction paper and cut out the shape. Decorate as desired with markers or crayons, then glue the paper to the frame.

A length of yarn or even a strip from a plastic grocery bag makes a great tail for a kite. Simply attach with tape at one corner of the frame. To fly your kite, tie a length of string to the center of the crossbar. Wait for a windy day, then find an open area to test out your kite. With a little bit of luck, you'll have it in the air in no time!

At its most basic, a kite is a very simple structure, but there are plenty of variations in how kites are made and the materials that can be used to build them. Help older children do research into different kinds of kites (box kites, for example) and building materials, such as wooden dowels or drinking straws for the frame and cloth for the covering on the frame. The possibilities are endless!

SWIMMING POOLS, A BREAK FROM SCHOOL, AND THE BLAZING SUN . . .

It must be summer!

· ·

Sure, the sun is shining and heat waves are rising up from the streets—but don't let the heat get you down! With kids out of school, families have more time than ever to spend together. Make the most of it with super fun activities that might have you breaking a sweat—but never breaking the bank.

27 **I SCREAM, YOU SCREAM!**
MAKING ICE CREAM IN A CAN

COST: $

MATERIALS: 2 clean differently-sized metal cans with tight-fitting lids (such as coffee cans), duct tape, milk, sugar, vanilla extract, rock or kosher salt, ice, flavorings (optional)

Homemade ice cream is one of summer's most indulgent and delicious treats. Even if you don't have an ice cream machine, this simple technique will allow you to make ice cream at home and burn some calories off while you do it.

In the smaller can, mix together 1 cup cold milk, ½ cup sugar, and 1 tsp. vanilla extract. You can also add flavoring, such as 1 Tbsp. of chocolate syrup, to your ice cream if you like. Experiment to create your favorite flavors. Strawberries, peaches, or candy pieces make excellent flavors as well.

Seal the can, tape it closed, and place it inside the larger can. Pack ice and rock salt in layers in the empty space between the two cans. Seal and tape the larger can and start shaking! Holding the can to shake it can make for some very cold fingers, so it might be fun to have the whole family sit on the ground and roll the can from person to person. It will take about 30 minutes for the ice cream to thicken, so make the rolling into a game.

SOME GAME IDEAS:

• See who can roll the can the farthest.
• Roll the can from person to person in alphabetical order.
• Roll the can from youngest to oldest, tallest to shortest, or in any other order you can think of.

For extra ice-cream fun, set up a sundae bar with all the fixings when the ice cream is ready to eat. You'll be screaming for this ice cream all summer long!

 FOR LARGER GROUPS OR PARTIES, HAVE GUESTS BRING THEIR OWN CANS. THEN THEY'LL HAVE THEIR OWN INDIVIDUAL ICE CREAM!

Sidewalk chalk is not expensive to buy, but it's a lot more fun to play with if you make it yourself. The ingredients you need to make the chalk can be found at your local craft store, and the recipe is a snap. All you need to do is mix the following together in a medium bowl:

- 1 cup plaster of paris
- 1 cup water

If you want to make a larger batch of chalk, simply mix more water and plaster of paris—as long as you mix equal proportions, your chalk will turn out just fine.

To tint your chalk, divide the mixture into smaller bowls. Add powdered tempera paint to make the colors you want. Once you have the colors you want, use tape or a rubber band to fasten waxed paper around one end of a toilet paper tube. Stand the tube, waxed paper side down, on a cookie sheet and pour one color of chalk in each mold. It will take the chalk about 24 hours to dry completely.

Once dry, peel away the paper tube and waxed paper and head outside to create your masterpieces! Draw family portraits or design hopscotch boards. The whole neighborhood will want to join in on the fun.

 AS YOU MIX IN THE TEMPERA PAINT, TALK TO YOUR CHILDREN ABOUT PRIMARY COLORS AND HOW TO USE THEM TO CREATE SECONDARY COLORS.

29 DANCE, DANCE, DANCE!

COST: **FREE**

MATERIALS: your family's favorite music, music player

Shake, shake, shake . . . shake, shake, shake! Dancing is a great way to have fun, burn some energy, and enjoy time together as a family. Putting together a family dance party takes almost no effort and is sure to put everyone in a good mood.

You can have a dance party at any time of day, but after dinner, when the entire family can be together, is often a nice time to groove. Before dinner, have everyone in the family choose at least one favorite song. The songs can be fast or slow, happy or silly—it's nice to have some variety. After dinner, push the furniture back to create as big a dance floor as possible and crank the tunes.

Adults sometimes feel inhibited by dancing, but kids have no qualms about expressing themselves through movement. If you feel self-conscious, watch your kids and copy their movements. Imitation is the sincerest form of flattery, and kids will love that you're following their lead. You can dance individually, in couples, or as a group.

SOME IDEAS TO KEEP THE PARTY HOPPING:

- sing along while you dance
- do the conga through the house
- show your kids dance classics such as the chicken dance, the twist, or the mambo
- give out awards like "Silliest Dancer" and "Most Graceful Movements"

On a hot day, nothing cools you off quite like playing with water or ice. Splashing around is fun on its own, but chipping away at an ice block filled with buried treasure is even better.

This activity requires some advance preparation. All you need is water and small objects such as super-bouncy balls, tiny plastic animals, spare change, or even jellybeans. Place a few toys in the bottom of a plastic container and barely cover them with water. Freeze this layer, then repeat until you run out of toys or space in the container. You can make one big icy treasure block for the whole family to chip away at or you can make smaller, individual blocks.

Once the blocks are frozen solid, take them outside, unmold them, and start chipping away to release the goodies within. You can use all kinds of tools to get to the treasures: child-sized hammers, spoons, spray bottles, or just let the sun do the work for you.

Who can get the treasures out the fastest? Who can get all the treasures, but leave the most ice intact? Who can come up with the most creative way to melt the ice? Teach your children about estimation by freezing a handful of pennies into the block and having them guess how many there are. For older children, freeze a variety of change and have them guess the total amount of money frozen in the block. The person who is closest gets to keep the change!

Summer's sunny skies and longer days draw everyone outdoors. Taking a walk as a family is a great way to spend time together and get some exercise. Why not give the experience more meaning and participate in a charity walk? Many walks are 5K (3.2 miles), a distance kids can manage (although the littlest ones might need a ride in the stroller), and some events even offer abbreviated kids' versions that are only a mile or so long.

You can research charity walks in your area on the Internet or in your local paper. If your family already has a cause or causes that you support, call the local offices and find out if they have a fundraising walk. If not, choose a cause that means something to your family. Do you want to help families who don't have enough to eat? Do you know someone who has battled cancer or who has autism?

Groups that sponsor walks make it easy to do fundraising. You can set a family goal and walk as a team. Work together to write a letter asking friends to support your cause. Pictures and personal stories are good ways to get people to respond. On the day of the walk, wear sturdy shoes and comfortable clothes and bring a water bottle. At many events, each participant is given a T-shirt commemorating the experience. You can be sure that everyone in the family will wear those shirts with pride. Go, team!

Children—and, let's face it, most adults—love the romantic notion of searching for hidden treasure. Letterboxing is a way to indulge that desire as a family. This activity involves following a series of clues to a hidden box, inside of which hides a rubber stamp. When you find this treasure, use it to stamp your "passport," a notebook you keep just for letterboxing. Continually growing in popularity, letterboxes are hidden all over the United States by people just like you. In fact, you've probably walked past hidden boxes without even knowing it!

To begin, visit www.letterboxing.org or check your local library for letterboxing resources. Either of those options will quickly provide you with a list of clues leading you to boxes in your area. The clues range from simple to complex, but do not require the use of specialized GPS equipment to follow. Once you've chosen a set of clues, set out with your passport, a stamp pad, and some snacks to find your treasure.

Searching for letterboxes will likely get your family to explore parts of your city or town that you've never seen before. In addition, the activity provides kids excellent practice in following directions and working together as a team. If you find that you get really involved with letterboxing, you may want to hide a box of your own and write up a series of clues leading to it. You may also find that when you visit friends or family in other towns, you add letterboxing to your list of "must-dos." Before you know it, you'll need to add new pages to your passport!

Who can resist a warm, soft pretzel? You can make these at home with very little effort and a whole lot of fun.

The easiest way to make pretzels is to buy ready-made pizza dough from your local pizza shop or grocery store. Preheat your oven to the temperature recommended on the package of dough. While the oven preheats, shape your pretzels. Sprinkle your kitchen counter or table liberally with flour, then break off chunks of dough to shape. Form pretzels into the traditional twisted shape, or make letters, numbers, or geometric designs. Just don't get tied up in knots!

Place your shaped pretzels on a cookie sheet. For a traditional pretzel, sprinkle the sheet with coarse cornmeal beforehand. Brush your pretzels with butter and sprinkle with salt. For a sweeter treat, dust with cinnamon sugar in place of the salt. Pretzels make a wonderful snack after a game of tag in the backyard or a weekend softball game. They pack well for day trips, too.

If you're feeling adventurous, you can make your own pretzel dough from scratch. Basic recipes can be found on the Internet or in many cookbooks. Budding chefs will love exploring the science of working with yeast and the magic of watching dough rise. Encourage your kitchen scientists to explore the chemistry behind yeasted dough—you might even learn something!

✳ FOR EXTRA FLAVOR, SEARCH FOR WHOLE-WHEAT OR HERB-INFUSED DOUGH.

"One person's trash is another person's treasure," or so the old saying goes. Put this theory to the test as you spend time together as a family and help make your neighborhood more beautiful.

Take a few minutes to plan a walking route through your neighborhood's streets. Then head out for your stroll, but take plastic bags and gloves with you because you're on a mission! As you walk, keep your eyes peeled for litter. You might be surprised—and distressed—by how much litter you find. This is a good time to talk to children about why littering is not kind and, in the bigger picture, what happens to things that we put in the trash. Collect the litter you find in your trash bags and take it home to throw out with the next garbage collection. Don't forget to separate what can be recycled from the true trash.

If you're having a hard time selling your kids on picking up trash for fun, turn the event into a contest. See who can pick up the most trash, who can find the coolest thing, and who can find the grossest thing. If you are lucky enough to live in an area where you don't have much luck finding litter, count your blessings and enjoy the weather. The question to ask when you get home is this: did you find any treasures among the trash?

All the world's a stage . . . and your whole family can be actors in the play. Staging a favorite story or book is a wonderful creative outlet for kids and adults alike.

The first thing you'll need to do is choose the story to act out. What are your family's favorites? If you choose a long, complex book, you might need to narrow your selection down to one scene so as not to get overwhelmed by the process. Choose who will play which roles. If you have more roles than family members, invite friends to join in. You can even put your pets in costume, too.

Use items from around the house to make your costumes. Towels and sheets can be capes, and everyday clothes can be combined in creative ways. If one member of the family has a particular flair for dress-up, you can name him or her costume designer.

Your production can be scripted or improv. You're just doing this for fun, so don't stress about rehearsing or memorizing lines. Roll with the punches and see where the scene takes you. You might end up with a version of the story that you like better than the original! If so, offer to put on your production for the neighbors in your own version of outdoor summer theater. Break a leg!

Puppets let kids and adults try on different personas and get creative. There are a variety of easy ways to make puppets that will engage the whole family.

HERE ARE THREE SIMPLE PUPPET IDEAS:

- Glue paper plates on craft sticks then use art supplies to create a face on each plate. This is a simple way for even the youngest members of the family to get involved since they can draw a basic happy face, sad face, angry face, or animal face on the plate and feel a sense of accomplishment with their independence.
- Use art supplies to create a puppet out of a paper lunch bag. Glue on ears to make an animal or make a super-silly monster using yarn for hair. Let your imagination run wild!
- Every household has lone socks hanging around in the laundry room. Turn them into sock puppets! Use a hot glue gun to attach decorations or draw features with fabric markers.

The great thing about puppets is that creating them is only half the fun. Once you have a gaggle of puppets, use them to stage puppet shows. The living room couch can be your stage. Let kids perform for adults and adults perform for kids. Your puppets can do improv comedy or act out fairy tales. They can even lip synch to favorite songs. Whatever you want—after all, you're pulling all the strings!

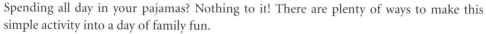

37   IT'S PAJAMA DAY!   COST: **FREE**   MATERIALS: pajamas

Spending all day in your pajamas? Nothing to it! There are plenty of ways to make this simple activity into a day of family fun.

Start by wearing your favorite pajamas, of course. Nothing else will do. If you have crazy slippers, even better. Be sure to do this on a weekend so that parents can participate, too. What kinds of things—other than sleep—do you usually do while wearing your pj's? It can be a fun change of pace to do them during daylight hours.

SOME IDEAS:

- Read stories to each other, including childhood favorites.
- Watch a movie.
- Take a bubble bath.
- Play board games or charades.
- Snuggle under a blanket with a favorite stuffed animal.
- Look through family photo albums.

Some regular day-to-day activities will suddenly be fun simply because you are wearing pajamas. Need to run a few errands? There's no reason that the kids—and brave adults—can't tag along in pj's. Get the mail in your bathrobe! And there's no better way to end the day than by sitting down to breakfast for dinner. The best part is that you're already dressed for bed. Sweet dreams!

Cool water on a hot summer day . . . what could be more refreshing? Rather than just running through the sprinkler (although that's always fun), exercise some creativity and paint the afternoon away with nothing more than water and a few household supplies.

It may sound crazy in its simplicity, but "painting" with water is lots of fun. Gather up brushes of different sizes, sponges, spray bottles, and bowls or containers of various sizes for the water. Head outside to the driveway, sidewalk, or wooden fence and start painting. The sun will evaporate your work, so if you don't like your creation, just wait a bit and try again!

Not sure what to paint? Plan a large work ahead of time and then work quickly as a team to complete it before it fades away. Or, paint a series of smaller scenes to create a story frame by frame. You can also play tic-tac-toe or paint a giant game of hopscotch. Since you're just working with water, you can even paint each other! Paint words onto bare forearms or legs and see if you can guess what's being spelled out.

If the allure of water paint wears off, you can also easily mix up paint that will last until it's washed away with the hose or the next hard rain. The recipe is simple: one part water to one part cornstarch plus a few drops of food coloring. Create semi-permanent masterpieces to wow your neighbors. Need a change? Rinse it away and start all over.

 BE CAREFUL WITH THE FOOD COLORING! IT CAN STAIN SOME PLASTIC AND WOOD SURFACES, BUT WILL BE FINE ON CONCRETE AND ASPHALT.

39

A "BEACH" IN YOUR BACKYARD

COST: $-$$

MATERIALS: buckets and other plastic containers, sand and water toys

The beach is just sand, water, and sun . . . yet it is the embodiment of summer. But most of us live far away from those sandy shores. Since the weather brings plenty of sunny days, all you need to bring the beach to your home is sand and water.

Commercial sand and water tables do the job, but they can be prohibitively expensive. You can make one at home that's just as fun. All that's required is a selection of buckets or large plastic containers, sand and water toys, your garden hose, and some sandbox sand (available at your local hardware store). In place of sand, you can use rice or dried beans, although building sand castles will be a bit more of a challenge! If sand is hard to come by, you can always use dirt from the backyard to create gloriously messy mud pies and mud sculptures.

Bring your containers out into the driveway or yard. Sand will work best placed in a larger, shallower container, although it's fun to fill a few deeper containers, too, for digging holes. You'll be surprised by how much fun everyone has splashing, pouring, and transferring water and sand from container to container. If you end up having a water fight with the hose, all the better. Just remember the sunscreen and enjoy your day at the "beach."

ORANGE PUMPKINS, FALLING LEAVES, AND COOL NIGHTS . . .

It must be fall!

Fall is a busy time of year. The kids are back in school and with seemingly back-to-back holidays, families are often hosting relatives or traveling to visit relatives. But don't let the hustle and bustle of fall keep you from spending time together as a family. With easy, fun activities, hanging out together will become the highlight of the season—and you won't have to spend a lot of money.

40

THE APPLE OF YOUR EYE
MAKING HOMEMADE APPLESAUCE

COST: $

MATERIALS: apples, cinnamon, large pot

Criss-cross, applesauce . . . Nothing says *fall* like the warm smell of apples and cinnamon. Making applesauce at home is a healthy way to enjoy a delicious autumn treat.

Getting the apples can be part of the fun of making the applesauce. If you live in an area where apples are grown, check the Internet or your local paper for nearby u-pick orchards. The cost of picking apples is comparable to buying them at the store, but the experience of going out to the orchard in the crisp fall air can't be beat. If there are no orchards nearby, don't despair. Applesauce made from store-bought apples will taste just as good.

To make the best applesauce, choose apples that are naturally sweet such as red delicious, gala, or rome. You can use all one type of apple or a mix. Peel, core, and quarter about 3 lbs. of apples, or 10 to 12 medium pieces of fruit. Kids can help peel the apples with a vegetable peeler.

Once that work is done, put the apple pieces in a large, heavy pot and add about one inch of water to the bottom. Cover and bring to a boil, then reduce the heat and let the apples simmer until very tender, about 20 minutes. Let the apples cool a bit, then mash right in the pot with a potato masher. Kids love to help with this step!

✳ FOR EXTRA FLAVOR, ADD A HANDFUL OF RAISINS OR DRIED CRANBERRIES TO YOUR APPLES AS THEY COOK.

Adjust the flavor of your applesauce to suit your family's taste. You might want to add a bit of white or brown sugar for extra sweetness or a few drops of lemon juice for brightness. Cinnamon is another popular addition to applesauce. Mix in your flavors of choice, then enjoy your healthy, homemade snack for breakfast, lunch, or dinner. Your applesauce will keep for about two weeks in the refrigerator, although it will almost certainly be gone long before then. *Bon appétit!*

41

THERE'S NO PLACE LIKE A HOME THEATER

COST: FREE

MATERIALS: one of your family's favorite films on DVD, snacks

Lights, camera, action! Going to the movies as a family is lots of fun, but it can be prohibitively expensive—even if you go on bargain night or to a matinee screening. One way to get around this is to go the extra mile when watching movies at home.

Rather than simply putting the movie in the DVD player and pressing play, turn a movie screening into a whole evening of fun. If you're feeling crafty, create paper tickets to be sold in a living room "box office." At dinner, discuss your movie selection. Who are the main characters? What are the basics of the plot? What do you think the ending will be like?

On the night of the screening, change into pajamas and break out the sleeping bags and blankets. Make sure you have everyone's favorite snacks on hand. Popcorn is a movie viewing must-have, but since you're at home, you can have any of your favorites for a fraction of the cost you'd pay at the theater. For a true theater experience, check to see if your employer owns a projector that you can borrow to screen the movie "theater-style" in large format on a blank wall.

Another advantage of being at home is the ability to stop and pause. Need a bathroom break? No problem! If no one seems to like the film, choose another. Didn't understand a scene? Replay it. Watch scenes you love over and over. Once the movie is over, rate it from one to four stars. Keep a family movie log so that you can refer back to your favorites. Dim the lights and mute your cell phones—it's showtime!

When you're racing through town in the car, buzzing from one destination to the next, you often don't notice the details whizzing by. Do you know what color the neighbors' houses are? How many blocks is it to the nearest park? Is there a fire hydrant on your street?

Getting out and about on bikes is a great way to enjoy the scenery while getting some exercise at the same time. Dust off your helmets and hit the road! Some kids might prefer to zoom around on scooters or hitch a ride in a bike trailer—whatever works for your family is fine.

No extensive planning is needed for this ride—you can simply take turns deciding which way to go at each fork in the road. Just be sure that someone knows how to get home! As you enjoy your ride, play a simple game of "I Spy." Take turns calling out sensory details about the sights, smells, sounds, feelings, and even tastes of your journey. It's easy to point out a red house, but try to pick out more subtle points of your trip. Can you hear an insect buzz in your ear? Feel the warmth of the sunshine on your face? Smell burning leaves? What does the crisp, fall air taste like?

When you get home, draw pictures that describe your journey. If you'd like, cut pictures from magazines that describe all your sensory experiences: sight, smell, taste, sound, and feel. Take the same trip again in the spring and compare your outings. Which sense got the biggest workout?

LOVELY LEAVES
MAKING STAINED "GLASS" WINDOWS

COST: **FREE-$**

MATERIALS: waxed paper, leaves, towels, iron, scissors

Who says that the glory of fall colors has to be limited to a few weeks in October? Enjoy the beauty of autumn leaves all year round by making them into your very own stained glass windows. All you need for this activity are leaves, waxed paper, and an iron.

Go on a leaf hunt to find the prettiest leaves in your neighborhood. Try to gather a variety of colors, shapes, and sizes. If you see other interesting items—such as flowers or pine needles—pick those up, too. They just need to be relatively flat. If you live in an area without fall foliage, you can do this activity with flowers, green leaves, or even crayon shavings!

HERE ARE THE STEPS TO CREATE YOUR OWN WINDOWS:

1. At home, sort through your treasures. Make sure they are clean and dry.

2. Remove thick stems.

3. Lay a sheet of waxed paper out on a towel on a large, flat surface. (The kitchen table makes a great workstation.)

4. Arrange your leaves on the paper, then lay another sheet of waxed paper over your creation.

5. Top with another towel, then iron on high heat to fuse together the two sheets of waxed paper.

6. Neaten up ragged edges with scissors, then hang in the windows to enjoy in the coming months.

Making your own playdough is easy, fun, and delightfully messy. The whole family can enjoy the process and the results. You don't even have to turn on the stove to make the dough. Get ready to mold, roll, and sculpt!

FOR EACH PERSON YOU WILL NEED:

- 1 cup all-purpose flour
- ¼ cup salt
- 1 tablespoon oil (any vegetable cooking oil is fine)
- ½ cup water

You can mix up one gigantic batch for the whole family, but children often like to make individual batches in smaller bowls. No matter which method you choose, start by mixing the flour and salt together. Add the oil and water, then use your hands to knead the ingredients together into a smooth ball of dough.

Now the real fun begins! Personalize your dough to make it just the way you want it. To brighten up your dough with food coloring, make a small well in the top of a ball of dough. Add a few drops of food coloring to the well, then knead the ball with your hands to mix in the color. You can even add a small scoop of glitter to the dough to make sparkle playdough. Or, make scented dough with the addition of a few drops of vanilla or peppermint cooking extract. Just remember that while your colorful, sparkly dough might look and even smell good enough to eat, it tastes *very* salty!

Parents who want to plan ahead can make a batch of playdough in the evening after the kids go to bed and hide drops of food coloring, glitter, or a small toy in balls of dough that are stored in individual zip-top bags in the fridge. In the morning, kids will delight in kneading their balls of dough to discover the secrets hidden inside.

Work together as a family to create all kinds of wonderful items with your dough. With a little imagination, you can make almost anything!

HERE ARE SOME PROJECT IDEAS:

- a barn and animals to live inside it
- a garden of playdough flowers
- long snakes that can then be rolled into coiled pots
- beads and charms (use a toothpick or knitting needle to make holes in the dough)

If you want to save your playdough masterpiece, leave it on a sunny windowsill to dry. If cracks form as the dough dries, fill them in with small bits of dough then paint over the repairs.

45 **VEGETABLE SCULPTURES** COST: **FREE-$**

MATERIALS: potatoes, toothpicks, bamboo skewers and/or chopsticks, carrots, raisins, sweet peppers, broccoli, olives, other veggies as desired

If you and your kids love Mr. Potato Head, you'll have a blast going *au naturel* in this edible activity. It's time to make a real Mr. Potato Head sculpture using healthy food you are likely to have on hand in your fridge and pantry. The potato sculpture is described here, but if you're feeling extra creative, make any kind of vegatable creature you can think of!

Each person making a potato head sculpture will need a large, raw baking potato. You'll also want to have a bunch of toothpicks and bamboo skewers handy.

HERE ARE SOME IDEAS TO GET YOU GOING:

- broccoli: the florets can be used for crazy hair or ears
- carrots: use whole carrots for legs, cut into matchsticks for decorations on clothing, or shave curls to make an edible carrot-top
- olives: black or green olives make great eyes
- raisins: use as eyes or decorations for clothing
- red, green, yellow, and orange pepper: strips can be made into shoes, or hollow out a whole pepper to use as a hat

Use the toothpicks and skewers to attach your decorations. Chopsticks can make great legs and arms. Don't limit yourself to the human form—animals and monsters are fun to create, too!

When your creations are complete, take some pictures for posterity. Then, pierce the potatoes a few times with a fork and pop them in the microwave. You can eat your sculpture for dinner!

COST: FREE-$

MATERIALS: clear plastic containers with lids, a variety of small objects that will fit in the bottle, uncooked rice, funnel

I spy with my little eye . . . The classic game of "I Spy" is fun for all ages. In this activity, "I Spy" goes miniature when an array of tiny objects is placed in clear plastic bottles or jars then hidden in rice.

This activity may sound simple, but it's guaranteed to provide hours of fun. The first thing you need to do is collect a variety of clean, clear plastic bottles with lids. Sports drink bottles and old mayonnaise jars work well. Then collect things to put inside.

SOME IDEAS:

- small plastic animals or people
- stickers
- beads
- loose change
- tiny balls
- bottle caps
- paper clips

Keep a list as you add the items to the bottle so that you know what to look for later. Once you've finished adding objects, use a funnel to fill the bottle about ¾ full with uncooked rice. Use a piece of string to tie the list of objects to the neck of the bottle. Now twist and turn the bottle to see if you can find everything inside! Alternatively, one person can keep the list while another person tries to make a list of all the treasures hiding in the bottle. What do you spy with your little eye?

Spending time with grandparents can be a joyful activity for the whole family. But not all families are lucky enough to be able to spend regular time with Grandma and Grandpa.

One wonderful way to bring the joy of the grandparent/grandchild relationship to your life (as well as someone else's) is to volunteer at a retirement home. Many retirement home residents rarely, if ever, get visitors, and nothing will brighten their day more than the sight of friendly faces—especially children—stopping by to say hello.

Look up local retirement facilities in your telephone book or online and call to see if they have volunteer opportunities. If there is a time that you can go visit, plan ahead by thinking about the kinds of questions you could ask the people you meet. Retirement home residents often love to talk about their childhoods.

While being a good listener is one of the kindest things you can do for someone who lives in a retirement home, there are plenty of other ways you can help residents. Offer to read or do crossword puzzles with those who have a hard time with those tasks on their own. Play card games or do puzzles. What are your family's favorite songs? Offer to sing them to the residents. Does anyone in the family play an instrument? Ask the staff if you could give a brief family recital. Your visits will bring the past to life for you and give the residents a breath of fresh air—it's a win-win.

HERE ARE SOME IDEAS TO GET YOU STARTED:

- Where did you grow up?
- How many siblings do you have?
- What was your life like as a child?
- What were your favorite things to do when you were little?
- What is your fondest childhood memory?

A DAY IN OUR FAMILY'S LIFE

COST: $-$$

MATERIALS: camera, photo albums, crafting supplies, computer (optional)

Kids and adults love to page through family albums and scrapbooks. It's fun to reminisce about places you've been and events you've celebrated. Sometimes, though, it's the little moments that make the best memories. Wouldn't it be fun to document a day in your family's life and make an album of the everyday events that make it special? Say "cheese!"

THERE ARE A FEW WAYS TO GET YOUR ALBUM READY:

1. Have each person take a turn carrying the family camera around for a day.
2. Have each family member carry around a disposable camera on the same day.
3. Take turns being the photographer on a day your family spends together.

Document anything and everything, from early-morning bed head to antics at the bus stop to what you eat for dinner. Once you have your photos, each member of the family can make an individual album or you can compile one family "day of" book. Organizing the photos offers everyone a chance to showcase his or her talents. Maybe someone is great at putting the photos in order, another writes witty captions, and another is page layout whiz. Play to everyone's strengths, and don't feel like you have to make a masterpiece—unless you want to, of course. You can even go digital—all kinds of software exists to organize the photos in your computer, make slide shows, and even create basic Web pages. The technologically savvy will love this option.

If your family enjoys making mini-albums, you might want to start documenting other events, like holidays, birthdays, or even trips to the zoo. You'll be glad you did. Photo albums make great gifts . . . and great memories.

ZOO

I saw a beautiful horse and named it Bella. It was a miniature race. Later we had Malli Cola. It tasted like a banana split and it is my favorite treat.

"Waste not, want not," or so the adage goes. It's not possible to avoid throwing some things away. But have you ever considered that there are some things going into your trash that could be put to better use?

Composting is easy, educational, and hands-on. To start composting, all you need is a composting bin. These range from simple to complex, free to expensive. Do some research as a family to find out what will work best for you.

HERE ARE SOME TIPS:

- Check with your municipal government to see if there is a town-sponsored composting program. If there is, you might be able to get a composting bin free or at low cost through them.
- Look for bins at your local garden center. They will likely have a variety of low-cost options.
- Ultimately, any big plastic or wooden container with drainage holes in the bottom will do. A 4' x 4' container is ideal, but feel free to start smaller.

You should put your container in a location with a lot of sun, if possible. Then start filling it up! Remember, your composting bin needs a mix of high-nitrogen "green" items and high-carbon "brown" items. The following chart gives you an idea of what sorts of common household items are compostable.

GREEN	BROWN
tea bags	cardboard
grass clippings	paper egg cartons
fruit and veggie peels and cores	shredded paper
old flowers	sawdust
coffee grounds	old leaves, twigs, and branches

Just be sure you don't add any meat, dairy, or anything cooked or processed. You'll also need water. The compost should feel like a damp sponge. If it's too dry, the materials won't break down, so add water as needed. And you'll need to "turn" your compost, which simply means that you should stir it up once a week or so to expose different parts to air and sunlight.

Your compost shouldn't smell. If it starts to give off an ammonia odor, you have too much "green" in it—ease up on those items and the smell will go away. If your compost starts to smell like trash, it might be too wet.

When it looks dark and crumbly, your compost is ready to use. Mix it with the top layer of soil in your garden to nourish plants or spread it around the base of your bushes to feed them as they grow. Congratulations: you have just completed the circle of life!

Rock, paper, scissors . . . well, how about *glue,* paper, scissors? Folding and cutting paper is a simple activity, but you'll be amazed at the things you can create from such meager materials.

The youngest members of the family will enjoy working with scissors and will likely be happy to simply cut pieces of paper into smaller and smaller bits. Kids can then use those bits and a glue stick to make a basic collage.

The older members of the family can make more formal collages. The collages can be abstract or have a theme such as "Our Favorite Things," "Places We Want to Go," or "People We Admire." Old magazines and catalogs are filled with words and images that can be used to create collages.

If collage-making doesn't inspire, how about folding a paper airplane? All you need is a standard 8 ½" x 11" sheet of paper. Draw on your piece of paper before folding to create a bright and colorful airplane. Then in just five simple steps, your plane will be ready for takeoff!

Experiment with different weights of paper and different positions for the wing fold. What combination makes the most stable airplane? What makes the plane that will fly the farthest?

PAPER AIRPLANE DIAGRAM:

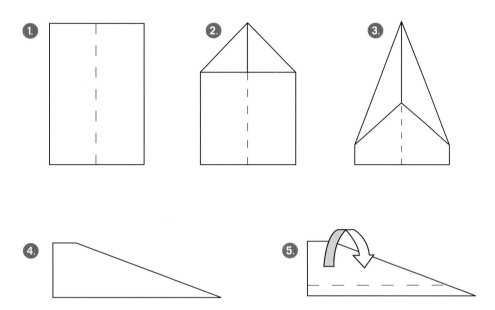

HERE'S WHAT TO DO:

1. Fold the paper in half lengthwise, making a hard crease. Unfold.
2. Fold the top corners down to meet at the center crease.
3. Fold the outer corners in to meet at the center crease again.
4. Fold the plane in on itself along the center crease.
5. Fold out the wings.

Traditional finger paints are a gooey mess that seem to end up on everything but the surface for which they are intended. While this finger painting activity is not mess-free, it's at least self-cleaning!

All you need for this activity is a few cans of shaving cream and an outdoor surface—like a picnic table or even a plastic tarp spread out on the ground. To paint, simply squirt the shaving cream onto your work surface and start painting with your hands. Everyone will find the squishy texture irresistible.

Kids will love helping to squirt out more cream; there's something undeniably fun about pushing the button, hearing that hiss, and watching the foam grow. Shaving cream is remarkably sturdy and can be used to create some sculpted effects, which will keep older children engaged. Use tools—like plastic cutlery or an ice cream scoop—to refine your creations. You can also mix four parts shaving cream to one part white glue to create textured paint. Just spread the mixture on paper and it will stay puffy when it dries, allowing you to create three-dimensional artwork.

Don't worry if everyone is covered in foam at the end of your activity. Head straight for the tub—you're already pre-soaped!

Remember the very first activity in this book? Go ahead and look back to refresh your memory . . . that's right, a time capsule! The end of the year is a great time to bring your capsule out of hiding and see how much has changed for your family since January 1.

Pick an evening and dedicate it to opening up your capsule. Do you remember where you hid it? Draw straws to see who gets to retrieve it and open it. Put on some of your favorite music and enjoy sifting through the contents from a year ago. You're likely to be surprised how much some things have changed and how much others have stayed the same.

You can reuse the time capsule container to make a new container to hide away. Or, once you're done inspecting your treasures, reseal the capsule and then create a new one for the next year. That way you'll have two to open after another year passes! Keep adding capsules to your collection—they make wonderful keepsakes. You can't save time in a bottle, but you can preserve some amazing family memories in your time capsules.

**If you and your family have enjoyed
these four seasons of fun,
we would love to hear from you.**

Please send your comments to:
Hallmark Book Feedback
P.O. Box 419034
Mail Drop 215
Kansas City, MO 64141

Or e-mail us at:
booknotes@hallmark.com